Adult Coloring Books

Inner Peace

Beautiful Images Promoting Mindfulness, Wellness, And Inner Harmony

Trendi Mindi

Copyright © 2016 by Trendi Mindi

ALL RIGHTS RESERVED. By purchase of this book, you have been licensed one copy for personal use only. No part of this work may be reproduced, use or redistributed in any form or by any means without prior written permission of the publisher and copyright owner.

Come Join Me!

Stay updated on my new arrivals.

www.trendimindi.com

I am thrilled to see you have purchased my one of my many books! I hope you get as much enjoyment out of them as I do creating them. I can guarantee my books will bring you peace and tranquility. Sit back, relax, and let your inner artist run wild.

Happy Coloring!

Trendi Mindi

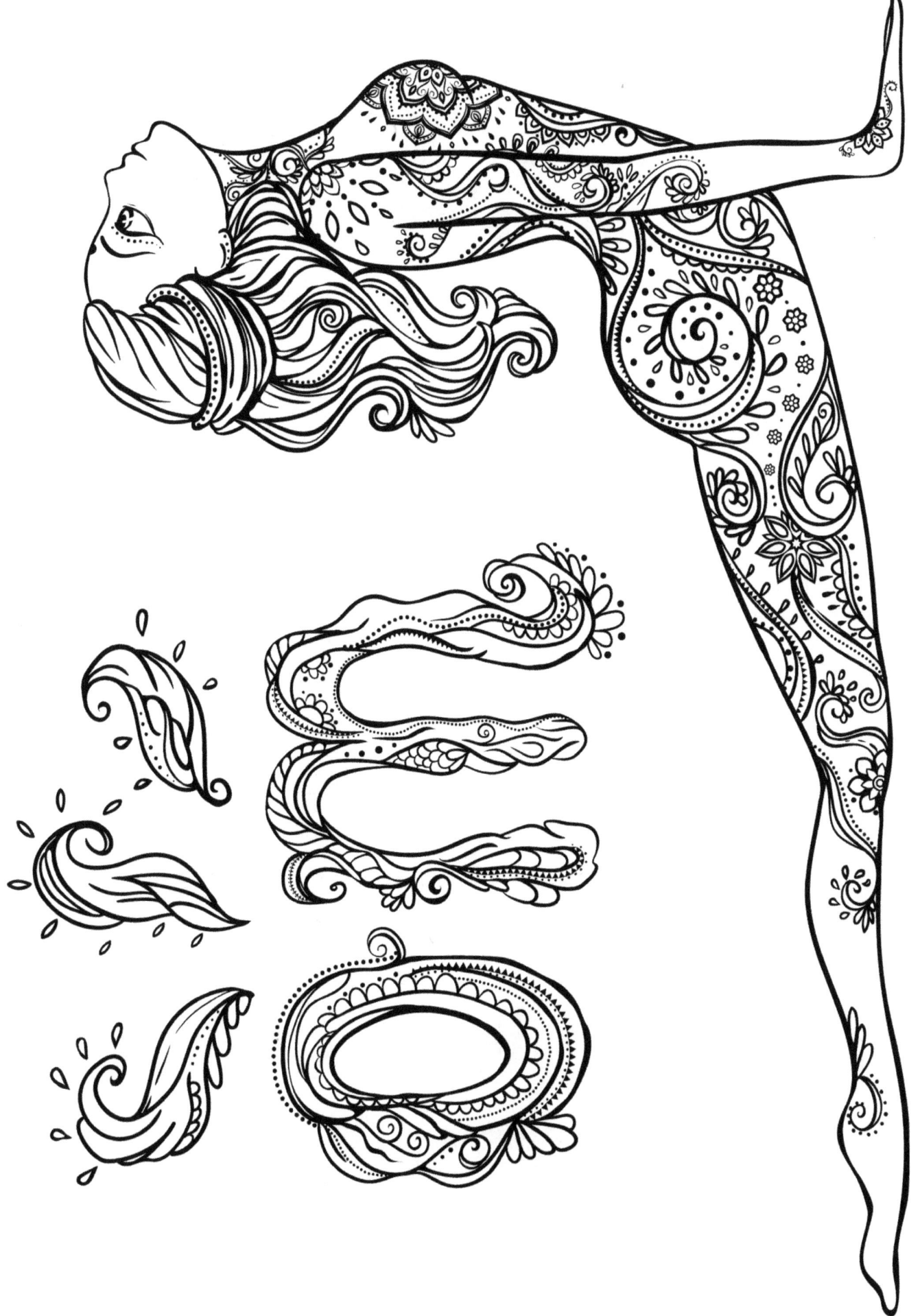

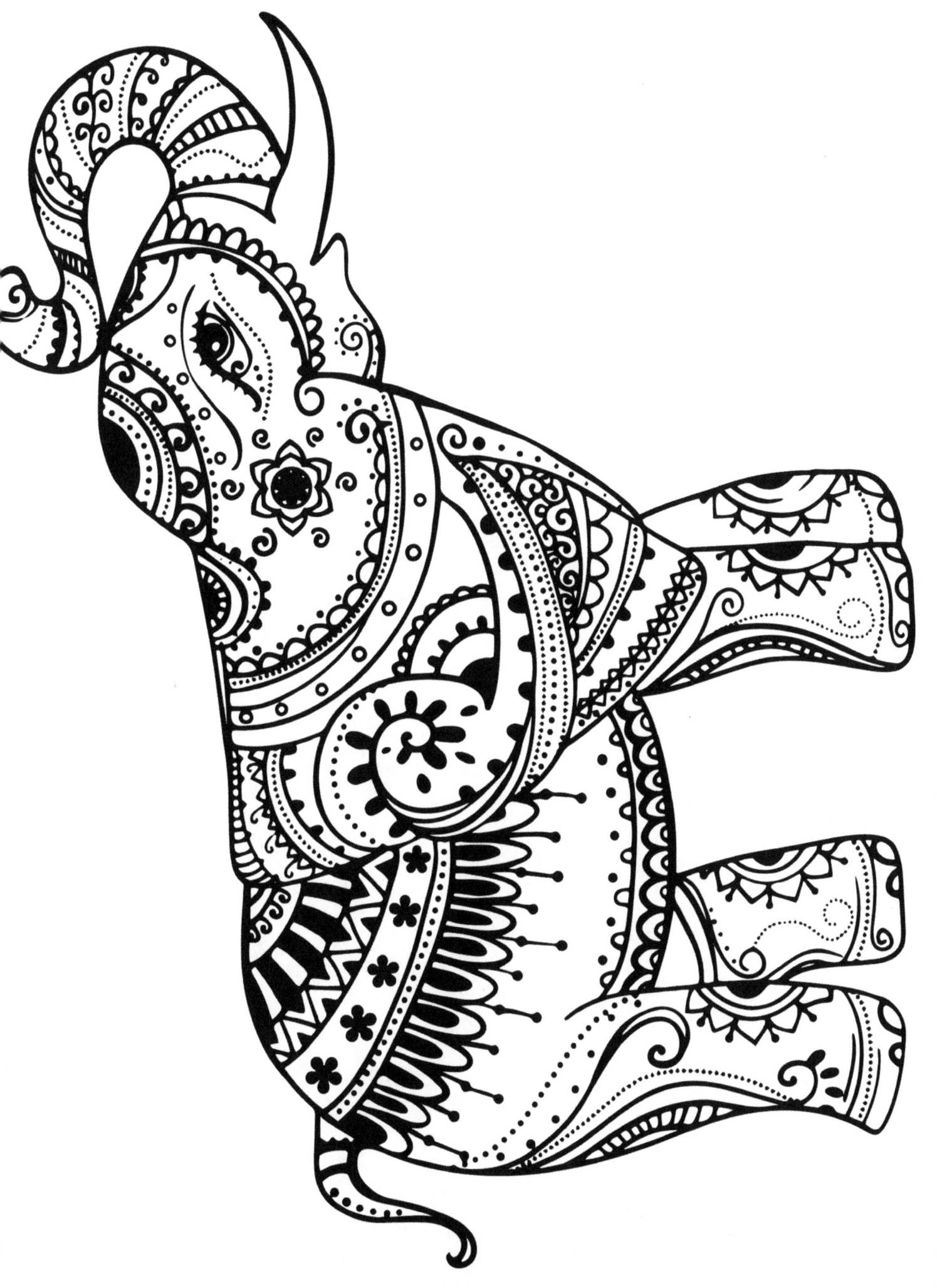

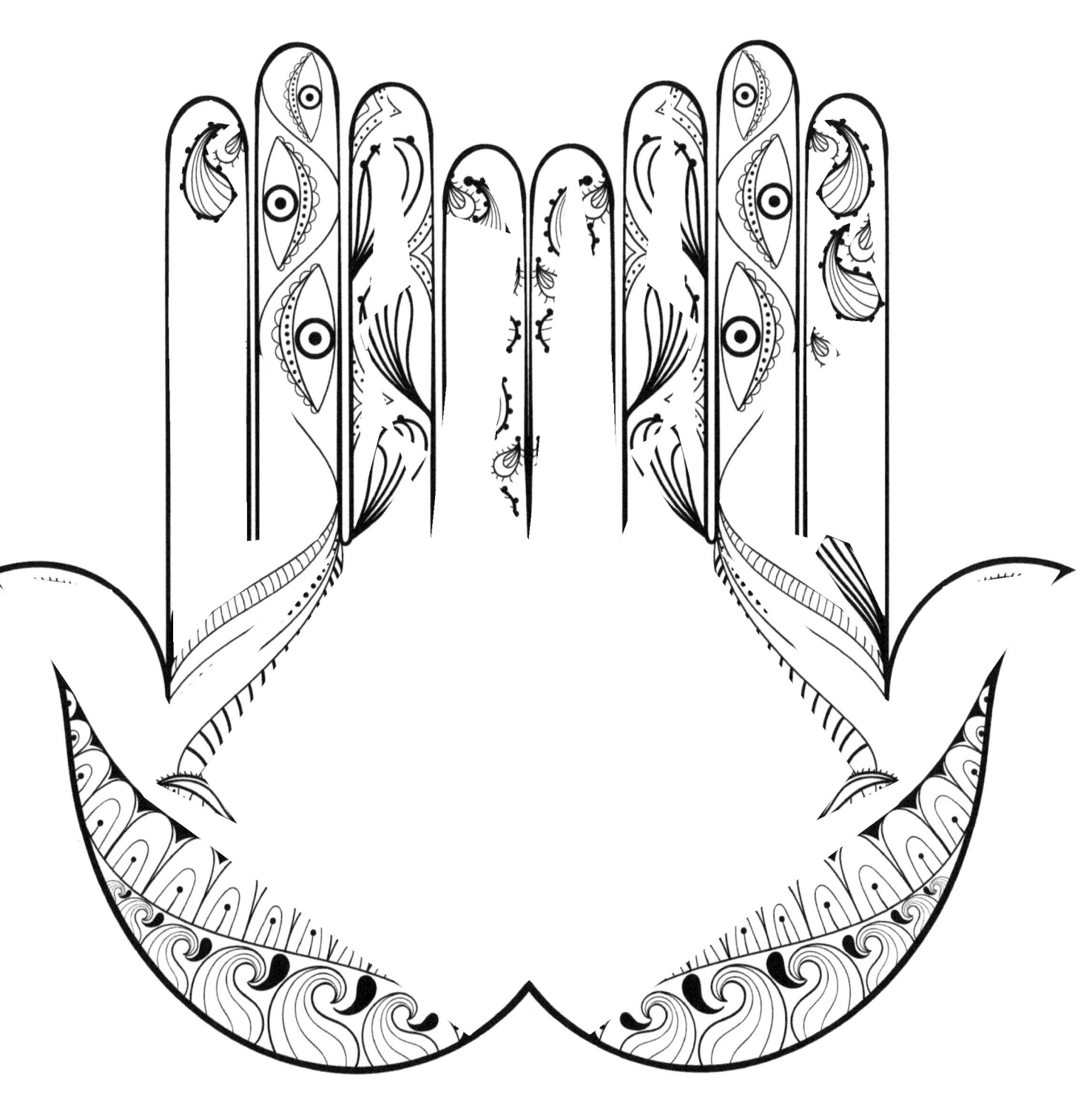

www.ingramcontent.com/pod-product-compliance
Lightning Source LLC
Chambersburg PA
CBHW081349040426
42450CB00015B/3361